Design: Niels Bonnemeier
Production: Patty Holden
Editors: Monika Römer, Gabriele Heßmann, Lisa M. Tooker
Food Editor: Lynda Zuber Sassi
Translation: Christie Tam

ISBN: 1-59637-075-0
Printed in China

Don't

special with *Carr's*®

Gregor Schaefer

Little

Cheese
and Wine

Contents

Unless otherwise indicated, all recipes make four servings.

Introduction

Cheese and Wine—
A Match Made in Heaven

Cheese and wine are two luxury items that each offer a broad range of flavor nuances and aromas, in their own, unique way. When the right cheese is pared with the right wine, the result is a harmony that warms the soul.

Deciding what goes together is a matter of personal taste and preference. Although there are several guidelines for combining cheese and wine, the truth lies in the individual palette.

The content in this book is meant to be a frame of reference that introduces the topic of pairing cheese with wine. A simple rule of thumb is that cheese and wine from the same geographical region will usually go well together. Such combinations have a basis in history. For example, a Munster cheese and Pinot Gris from Alsace are complementary; a Chaource cheese from the Champagne region meets its match when partnered with a dry Champagne.

Another rule of thumb is that wine and cheese are meant to complement, not overwhelm one another. For example, a mild cheese is best accompanied by a lighter wine. A semi-dry white wine is a good match for an acidic cheese. If the cheese has a distinctively tangy or salty flavor, its best partner may be a sweet wine or one with a high level of acidity. Young, fresh cheese harmonizes with sparkling, fruity wines. The stronger and richer the cheese, the more full-bodied the wine needs to be.

Contrary to the praises that Napoleon sang of the combination of Epoisses cheese with a mature, red Burgundy, the fact is that oftentimes, cheese is better suited accompanied by a white or dessert wine. Naturally, there are wonderful combinations of cheese and red wine, but many times white wines are the better match, because strong tannins and distinctive barrel notes in reds are not compatible with cheese. On the other hand, Stilton with an aged Port is a classic combination.

Yet another rule of thumb is that true flavor experiences are possible only when both the wine and the cheese are of the highest quality. A marginal quality cheese with a mediocre wine will simply not provide a memorable flavor adventure.

Other compatible flavor pairings to keep in mind include salty and sweet, i.e. a salty cheese is delicious with a sweeter wine. Bitter flavors in cheese are well-balanced by a sweet wine. An acidic wine will tend to accentuate bitterness in a cheese. Strong and hot spices can be pleasantly balanced by a sweet wine such as a later harvest Riesling or a Gewürztraminer, but are usually intensified to an unpleasant degree by an acidic wine. A tannic wine complements rich meaty dishes. When bitterness in wine (youthful tannins in young red wines) meets bitterness in food (radicchio, arugula, chicory, etc.), the result is undesirable and not at all palate pleasing. A much more pleasurable experience can be had by combining tannins with roasted flavors, which is why a young red wine is an ideal accompaniment to seared meat. Smokey foods also go well with "smoky" wine, i.e. wine aged in fire-toasted oak barrels.

Cheese Varieties

Cheese production requires rennet, an enzyme obtained from a calf's stomach and/or from byproducts of acidification processes, such as milk proteins. When added to fresh cow, goat, sheep or buffalo milk, these substances trigger a curdling process, known as "coagulation," resulting in the creation of a gelatinous mass. This "cheese curd" comprises protein and fat

from which the "whey" (the watery component of the milk) has separated. The end result depends on how the cheese curd is further processed.

First of all, the curd is cut by means of a "cheese wire" and separated from the whey. The finer the curd, the firmer the cheese. This mass is then pressed into the appropriate mold to allow additional whey to drain. Placed in a brine bath, the cheese starts to form a protective rind and becomes firm. The maturing process, which is influenced by bacteria, yeast and mold cultures, determines what the cheese will be like in its finished form. Most of these cheese making components exist naturally and are difficult to mass produce.

Roquefort is still only made in the original caves because they are the only place where the corresponding mold required for production is found.

During the ripening phase, which can range anywhere from one to over 12 months, the cheese is "cured," i.e. washed with whey and brine or brushed with red mold spores, depending on the type of cheese to be produced, the aromas desired and the desired structure of the rind.

A special category of cheese is called sour milk cheese (Harzer, Mainzer, etc.). In this case, the milk is coagulated using only lactic acid bacteria, without the addition of rennet. The ripening phase for sour milk cheese lasts only a few days. This type of cheese goes very well with a fresh, highly acidic wine, such as a Riesling from the Moselle region or a Sauvignon Blanc. In the end, the finished sour milk cheese is not sour at all.

MNFS and FDM

Cheese is divided into five categories based on "moisture in the nonfat substance" (MNFS): Fresh (e.g., Cantadou, feta, mascarpone, mozzarella and ricotta—over 73 percent moisture); soft (e.g., Camembert and Brie—over 67 percent); semi-soft (e.g., bonbel, fontina and Stilton—61–69 percent); semi-hard (e.g., Edam, Emmenthaler, Gouda, Gruyère and manchego—54–63 percent); and hard (e.g., Parmesan, pecorino and provolone—less than 56 percent).

Whereas the nonfat substance refers to the total cheese volume without the fat, the dry matter is the total cheese substance without the moisture component. The abbreviation FDM does not refer to the fat content of the cheese but only to the fat content of the "dry matter." To determine the absolute fat content of a cheese, you must also know its moisture content. For example, if a cheese weighs 3.5 ounces and its moisture component weighs 1.75 ounces; its dry matter also weighs 1.75 ounces. If this cheese has 50 percent FDM, the total fat content of the cheese is only 25 percent. Based on the defined moisture content of the five cheese categories, you can estimate the actual fat content of the various cheeses with relative accuracy using the following formula: Multiply the percentage number of the specified FDM by the following factors: Hard cheese by 0.7; semi-hard and semi-soft cheese by 0.6; soft cheese by 0.5; and fresh cheese by 0.3. As a general rule of thumb, you'll notice that the absolute fat content of cheese is a little more than half the FDM.

Apart from its dietetic aspects, this knowledge can also be used to select the right wine for a cheese. The lower the cheese's moisture content, the more concentrated its flavor and the more complex the accompanying wine should be. With a soft cheese, a simple, cool Frascati or rosé will do. A richer soft cheese such as Chaumes or Epoisses requires a fruity Pinot Noir or rich, full-bodied Chardonnay. Hard cheese such as pecorino is compatible with the richest white wines (for example, a dry Riesling) and big, mature red wines from Burgundy, Piedmont or Napa.

But that's enough theory. The recipes that follow will give you ideas about how to find good partners for cheese dishes where cheese plays a main role. Take them as inspiration for discovering your own favorite flavor combinations. As stated above, there are no hard and fast rules; they can all be bent to conform to your personal tastes and preferences.

—Cheers and bon appetite!

Appetizers

Countless delicacies can be prepared with cheese, whether as an opener to a fine meal, as adornment on a party buffet or simply as a small, between meal snack.

In conjunction with salad, cheese can provide a light and delicate flavor that does not spell the end of a meal. When selecting an appetizer, keep in mind the courses that follow. As far as the wine is concerned, start with something light and white so you'll have room to up the ante over the course of the meal. If a particular dish would work just as well with a white or red wine, go with the white and introduce the red in the next course.

Greek Peasant Salad with Feta

1/2 cucumber, 4 firm tomatoes, 2 small red onions,
1 green bell pepper, 1/2 cup black olives,
1 stalk fresh dill, 2 stalks Italian parsley,
1/2 cup extra virgin olive oil, 1/2 cup freshly squeezed
lemon juice, 3 1/2 ounces feta cheese, Kosher salt,
Freshly ground black pepper

Peel cucumbers and cut into thick slices. Remove cores from tomatoes and cut into wedges. Peel onions and cut into thin rings. Cut bell pepper in half, remove the stem, seeds and interior, and cut into strips. Arrange vegetables on a platter and top with olives.

Rinse the dill and parsley, pat dry, remove leaves and chop. Set aside.

In a cup, whisk together olive oil, lemon juice, salt and pepper, and drizzle over the salad. Crumble feta and sprinkle on top. Finally, top with dill and parsley.

Serve a well-chilled Sauvignon Blanc with this Greek salad. Its herbal quality is a good match for the salad's pungent flavors. An Italian Dolcetto's fresh, fruity acidity also works well.

Endive Salad with Roquefort

1 endive head, 3½ ounces Roquefort,
2 tablespoons extra virgin olive oil,
2 tablespoons walnut oil, 2 teaspoons white
wine vinegar, Pinch of sugar, ½ cup walnuts,
3 tablespoons butter, 12 baguette slices,
Kosher salt, Freshly ground black pepper

Clean endive, rinse and dry. Tear into bite-sized pieces and place in a bowl. Set aside.

Whisk together half the Roquefort with the olive oil, walnut oil, vinegar and sugar and season with salt and pepper.

Toast the walnuts on an ungreased pan. Chop 2 tablespoons into small pieces and set aside. Sprinkle remaining walnuts over the endive.

Combine the butter and remaining Roquefort until soft.

Toast the baguette slices until golden-brown, spread the butter and cheese on top and sprinkle with chopped walnuts.

Pour the dressing over the endive and toss. Serve with baguette slices on the side.

🍷 To do this salad justice, select a semi-dry Riesling, an Alsace Gewürztraminer or a Muscat.

Swiss Sausage Salad

8 ounces Swiss Emmenthaler,
8 ounces mild Italian sausage,
2–3 green onions, 1 tablespoon chives,
2 tablespoons red wine vinegar, Pinch of sugar,
1 teaspoon mustard, $1/3$ cup extra virgin olive oil,
Kosher salt, Freshly ground black pepper

Cut cheese and sausage into same-size matchsticks. Clean onions and cut into fine rings. Finely chop the chives. In a shallow bowl, combine cheese, sausage, onions and chives.

Whisk together the vinegar, sugar, mustard, oil, salt and pepper to make the dressing and drizzle over the salad.

Serve a hearty multigrain bread with butter on the side.

This dish goes well with a light red wine like a Gamay or Beaujolais that stand up to the cheese and sausage but don't overpower.

Gorgonzola Balls

½ red bell pepper, ½ cup chives,
14 ounces ricotta cheese, 7 ounces Gorgonzola,
⅓ cup Italian parsley, 15–20 cherry tomatoes

Remove stem, seeds and interior from bell pepper and chop finely. Rinse and finely chop the chives.

In a bowl, combine ricotta, Gorgonzola, chives and bell pepper. Refrigerate for 1 hour.

Remove the cheese mixture and moisten your hands. Shape cheese into small balls and place them on a baking sheet. Cover and refrigerate for 2 hours.

Rinse and finely chop the parsley, then spread it on a flat surface or plate. Remove the cheese balls from the refrigerator and roll them in the parsley until covered.

To serve, arrange cheese balls and cherry tomatoes on a platter. Garnish with additional chopped parsley.

🍷 A full bodied, complex Barolo will stand up nicely to this strong cheese. So will a rich and tannic Cabernet Sauvignon.

Onion Soup

3–4 medium yellow onions,
2 tablespoons butter, 1 tablespoon flour,
2 cups beef stock, 1 cup dry white wine,
1 teaspoon caraway seeds, 8 slices baguette,
4 ounces freshly grated Gruyère,
Kosher salt, Freshly ground black pepper

Peel onions and cut into fine rings.

In a Dutch oven, melt the butter and braise onion rings over low heat for about 15 minutes until tender. Stir occasionally, making sure the onions don't brown. Dust onions with flour, then add stock, white wine and caraway seeds, and season with salt and pepper. Cover and simmer over medium heat for about 10 minutes.

Preheat oven to 425°F.

Toast bread slices and place in the bottom of 4 oven-proof soup bowls. Place the bowls on a baking sheet. Pour the soup into each bowl over the bread and sprinkle with Gruyère .

Place the soup on the center oven rack for 5–7 minutes until the cheese melts and turns golden-brown.

Add a shot of cognac (about 1½ tablespoons), for a distinctively different flavor.

This hearty onion soup is well partnered with a mature, white, "spicy wine." The Gewürztraminers from Alsace are the best-tasting wines with this dish. For red wine, a Côtes du Rhone is a classic combination with the innate spice and peppery flavors, making a perfect companion to this rich soup.

Parmesan Flan

Makes 6–8 ramekins

$^1/_2$ cup butter, 3 tablespoons flour, 2 cups milk,
6 ounces finely grated Parmigiano-Reggiano, 3 eggs,
Butter for the ramekins, 2–3 pears for garnish

Preheat oven to 350°F.

Prepare a white sauce: Melt butter and stir in the flour until golden then add milk and stir vigorously until smooth. Remove from heat and stir in the Parmigiano-Reggiano until smooth. Add the eggs, stirring until thoroughly combined.

Carefully butter the ramekins and pour in flan mixture. Place ramekins in a hot water bath and bake on the center oven shelf for 25 minutes. If the mixture becomes too brown, cover with aluminum foil.

Remove ramekins and let cool for 10 minutes.

Cut the pears into quarters, remove the cores and slice finely.

To serve, reverse the flan onto individual plates and arrange several pear slices in a fan pattern beside each one.

📖 Drizzle aged Balsamico Tradizionale, which has a

honey-like consistency, over the top of this delicious dish. It is a rare delicacy.

As a substitute, drizzle a premium balsamic vinegar that has been reduced. Combine 1 cup balsamic vinegar, 1 tablespoon honey, 1 teaspoon fresh thyme leaves and 1 stalk rosemary. Bring to a boil and reduce to one third over low heat. Pour through a fine strainer and let cool. Keep this reduction in the refrigerator for as long as you would keep regular vinegar.

Serve a Pinot Grigio or an Italian Chianti, which is a natural favorite.

Bruschetta with Ricotta and Deep-Fried Parsley

3 large stalks Italian parsley, 1 small garlic clove,
2 large slices rustic country bread, 4 ounces ricotta,
3 tablespoons extra virgin olive oil,
Kosher salt, Freshly ground black pepper

Rinse parsley, pat dry and remove leaves. Finely chop one-third of the parsley. Peel garlic and slice in half. Lightly toast bread on both sides. Rub each slice of bread with a piece of garlic then spread the ricotta evenly on top.

In a pan, heat 1 tablespoon of oil and fry parsley leaves for 2–3 minutes. Divide the fried parsley in half and arrange on top of the bruschetta. Drizzle the remaining olive oil over the top, season with salt and pepper and sprinkle with remaining parsley.

Serve with a light to medium bodied fruity wine. A Viognier, Sauvignon Blanc or Gewürztraminer on the white side, or a Beaujolais, Pinot Noir or light Merlot, if you fancy a red.

Crostini with Four Cheeses

1–2 stalks celery, 2 ounces fontina cheese,
3 ounces Taleggio or other soft Italian cheese,
3½ ounces mozzarella, 5 fresh basil leaves,
12 small baguette slices,
1½ ounces grated Parmigiano-Reggiano,
Freshly ground black pepper

Preheat oven broiler.

Clean celery and slice thinly. Remove rind from fontina and Taleggio and dice. Dice mozzarella into same size pieces and combine celery with all cheeses in a bowl. Rinse basil, pat dry and chop finely.

Place baguette slices on a baking sheet and toast until golden. Arrange celery and cheese on top of the bread. Season with pepper and sprinkle with Parmigiano-Reggiano. Place under the broiler until the cheese starts to melt and turn golden. Remove from the oven and cool slightly. Sprinkle basil over the top and serve.

🍷 A Piedmont Dolcetto or a Bardolino are both fine choices to pour alongside Crostini with Four Cheeses.

Chèvre Chaud Wrapped in Bacon

8 bacon slices, 8 small, round fresh goat cheese
slices, 1 large tart apple (e.g., Granny Smith), Butter
for the pan, 1 tablespoon honey, 1 tablespoon
lemon juice, Coarsely ground black pepper

Preheat the oven to 400°F.

Slice each piece of bacon in half and wrap one half in
one direction around the goat cheese and the other half
around the other direction so that no goat cheese shows.

Peel the apple, remove core with an apple corer and
cut into 8 rings of equal size.

Thoroughly butter a baking pan and line with apple
rings. Drizzle honey over the top of each ring then
place 1 bacon wrapped goat cheese on the top. Bake on
the top oven rack for 10 minutes. Turn on the broiler
and brown for 2 more minutes. The bacon should be
crispy and the honey slightly caramelized.

Remove from the oven, sprinkle with a little pepper,
drizzle with lemon juice and serve immediately.

The cheese's sweet, sour and spicy aromas meet
their match with a rich, aged Gewürztraminer. A
hearty Riesling with a lot of residual sugar is also
compatible.

Fried Mozzarella Balls

8 slices sandwich bread,
1 mozzarella ball (5 ounces),
1 tablespoon chopped oregano,
2 eggs, 1/3 cup milk, 1/2 cup breadcrumbs,
3 tablespoons flour, Oil for deep-frying,
Kosher salt, Freshly ground black pepper

Cut the bread into eight 3-inch circles using a cookie cutter or the rim of a glass.

Slice mozzarella into 4 even pieces, placing each slice on top of a bread circle (the bread should be a little larger than the cheese). Season with oregano, salt and pepper, and top with remaining bread circles.

In a shallow bowl, whisk together eggs and 2 tablespoons of milk. Pour remaining milk into a shallow bowl. Spread breadcrumbs on a flat plate.

Dunk the edges of the bread in the milk and press together so that the cheese does not escape during frying, then roll in breadcrumbs. Dip both sides of the bread in the egg mixture and dust with flour. In a tall pan, heat the oil and deep-fry sandwiches until golden. Drain on paper towels and serve immediately.

🍷 This crispy mozzarella treat tastes great with a Sauvignon Blanc or Pinot Grigio.

Feta in Phyllo

6 ounces feta, 1 egg, 4 ounces cottage cheese,
$\frac{1}{2}$ cup chopped assorted herbs (e.g., chives, oregano
and parsley), $\frac{1}{2}$ cup butter, 10 sheets phyllo pastry

Preheat oven to 400°F.

Crumble feta and combine with egg, cottage cheese
and herbs. Set aside.

Melt the butter in a small saucepan. Prepare one dry
and one damp kitchen towel. Throughout preparation,
keep the pastry covered with both towels (dry on
bottom, moist on top); otherwise, it will dry out and
become brittle.

Line a baking sheet with parchment paper. Spread out
the first pastry sheet on a work surface. Brush pastry
with melted butter, place a second sheet on top and
cut into 4 strips of equal width. Place 2 teaspoons of
cheese filling at the narrow end of each strip. Brush
butter on the outside edges and start rolling up from
the cheese end. After 2 rotations, fold in the sides by
about $\frac{1}{2}$ inches to keep the filling from escaping and
continue rolling. Repeat this process with remaining
pastry strips and filling.

Place finished pastry rolls on the baking sheet with the
seam side down and brush the tops with remaining

butter. Bake in the oven for 8–10 minutes until golden-brown.

Phyllo pastry is available in most grocery stores, especially those that sell Greek, Turkish and Middle-Eastern foods. Buy it frozen in the form of a roll, thaw and unroll the thin pastry layers.

Prepare this appetizer a day ahead of time. Refrigerate or freeze the unbaked rolls. Feta in phyllo is delicious warm, cold or at room temperature.

For variety, vary the herb mixture. Instead of the specified herbs, use dill and mint, or replace the herbs with finely chopped shallots.

Serve this appetizer with a semi dry chilled Riesling or a light French rosé on a summer day. Or when the weather turns cooler, a Pinot Noir or Zinfandel will go nicely.

Vegetarian Entrées

Many delicious cheese dishes have been created in the European Alpine regions—for instance, Cheese Spätzle and Fonduta, a delicate cheese fondue from Piedmont. These specialties, as economical as they are satisfying, provide the warmth and strength that the traditionally hard-working people once needed to survive the cold and blustery winters. Today, a cheese fondue shared with a cozy circle of friends is still fun, whether you're in the mountains or a flatlander.

The wines of the Alpine regions offer an endless variety of flavor nuances that, apart from a few exceptions where beer might be the better choice, you can find the right wine for most any cheese dish. Taking into account personal taste, it's best to select the wine to match the dominant aroma of the particular dish, or on the basis of the flavor created when individual ingredients are combined.

If there are several wines that might go with the meal, base your choice on the main course. If, the main course is followed by another cheese course, save heavier wines for later courses and serve something milder with the entrée.

Penne Rigate with Spicy Cheese Sauce

1 small dried chile pepper, 1 clove garlic,
1 green onion, 1 tablespoon butter,
1 teaspoon fresh thyme leaves, 1 cup cream,
1/2 cup white wine or rosé, 2 cups penne rigate,
2 ounces freshly grated Bel Paese,
1 ounce freshly grated Parmigiano-Reggiano,
2 tablespoons chopped Italian parsley,
Kosher salt, Freshly ground black pepper

Cut chile pepper in half, remove seeds and chop finely.
Peel garlic and chop finely. Clean green onion and chop
into fine rings.

In a large pan, melt butter, add chile pepper, garlic and
onion, and braise briefly. Stir in thyme, cream and wine,
reducing to one third.

Cook penne in a large amount of salted water according to package directions until al dente, then drain.

Melt both types of cheese into the sauce and season
with salt and pepper. Add the penne and combine until
the pasta is thoroughly coated with the sauce. Sprinkle
with chopped parsley and serve immediately.

This creamy, spicy sauce cries out for a smooth
counterpart. Choose a Gavi di Gavi from Piedmont
or a well-chilled rosé from Côtes de Provence.

Macaroni and Cheese

2 cups milk, 1 tablespoon salt,
2 cups elbow macaroni,
8 ounces freshly grated Swiss cheese,
3 large onions, 4 cloves garlic, ½ cup butter

Preheat oven to 350°F.

In a pot, bring 1 cup of milk and salt to a boil and cook pasta according to package directions until al dente. Butter a baking dish. Layer the dish with pasta and remaining milk and sprinkle with cheese. Bake in the oven for about 10 minutes.

In the meantime, peel onions and chop the garlic. In a pan, melt the butter and sauté the onions and garlic until translucent, then add on top of the pasta.

🍷 A light Côtes du Rhône or a peppery Syrah make a great complement to this classic favorite. A smooth Riesling that's not too acidic is a fine white choice.

Cheese Soufflé

1 cup milk, 3 tablespoons butter, 3 tablespoons flour,
Freshly grated nutmeg, 4 egg yolks, 3 cups freshly
grated Comté or Gruyère, 5 egg whites,
Kosher salt, Freshly ground black pepper

Preheat oven to 350°F.

Briefly bring milk to a boil. In a heavy saucepan, melt butter and sauté flour. Remove pan from heat and stir in hot milk without allowing clumps to form. Season with nutmeg, salt and pepper. Simmer over low heat for about 2 minutes, then remove from heat. Add egg yolks and cheese, stirring until thoroughly combined. Beat egg whites until very stiff and carefully fold into the cheese.

Carefully butter a smooth-sided 8 cup baking dish or soufflé dish and add the cheese mixture. Bake on the bottom oven rack for 45 minutes until it becomes golden and has doubled in size. Serve immediately!

During the first 20 minutes, do not open the oven door, this will cause the soufflé to collapse.

On the side, serve a crispy mâche salad with bacon and croutons.

Pour a ripe, barrel-fermented French Chardonnay. Or, if you prefer a heavier red wine, serve a Chianti or Côtes du Rhône.

Potato Pancakes with Cheese

1 onion, 4 russet potatoes, 1 tablespoon butter,
1 cup vegetable stock, 14 ounces montasio cheese

Peel onions and chop finely. Peel potatoes and slice
into shoestrings. In a frying pan, heat butter and braise
onions. Add potatoes and toss until coated. Pour in
enough vegetable stock to barely cover the potatoes.
Simmer over low heat until tender, adding more stock
as necessary.

Cut cheese into fine slices. As soon as the potatoes are
tender and the stock has boiled away, sprinkle cheese
on top and melt slowly. When the pancake develops a
brown crust around the edges, remove from the pan
and serve hot.

🍷 This simple peasant dish from Umbria tastes best
with a simple, red, Italian table wine. A Pinot Noir
would also be good.

Risotto with Parmigiano-Reggiano

4 cups beef stock, 1 small onion,
2 tablespoons extra virgin olive oil,
1⅓ cups Arborio rice,
3 tablespoons freshly grated Parmigiano-Reggiano,
2 tablespoons softened butter, Kosher salt

Bring the stock to a simmer in a stockpot.

Peel and finely chop the onion. In a wide pot, heat the olive oil and sauté the onions until translucent. Add rice and sauté while stirring until the grains are coated with oil.

Add about ½ cup of simmering broth and boil over high heat while stirring constantly until all the liquid has boiled away. Repeat this procedure over a period of 15–20 minutes until the rice is done—it should have developed a creamy, soft consistency but still be firm.

About 1–2 minutes before the rice is done, add the grated Parmigiano-Reggiano and butter while stirring constantly until it melts and evenly coats the rice. If necessary, season with salt and serve immediately.

Although risotto with Parmigiano-Reggiano is delicious by itself, this Italian specialty is a fine foundation for other risotto variations. Try adding peas and ham, or asparagus or squash.

Risotto is compatible with a variety of wines provided they are not too acidic. Try a Pinot Grigio or Chardonnay. An Italian Brunello, made from the Sangiovese grape, offers a good balance of flavor to go with the risotto or a lighter Italian red like a Bardolino is a fine match.

Goat Cheese and Pine Nut Tart

1 cup white flour, ¹/₂ cup cold butter,
2 tablespoons sesame seeds,
1 small red bell pepper, 5 ounces chèvre,
1 large egg, ¹/₂ cup crème fraîche,
1 level tablespoon honey,
2 tablespoons pine nuts

Heap flour onto a work surface and make a well in the center. Cut the butter into small pieces and place them along with the sesame seeds and 1 tablespoon water in the well. Stir, then knead from the outer edges toward the center until the dough is smooth. Shape into a ball, wrap in plastic wrap and place in the refrigerator for 1 hour or in the freezer for 10 minutes.

Preheat oven to 425°F.

Cut the bell pepper in half, remove stem, seeds and interior, and bake in the oven until the surface turns black and blisters. Remove the skin and cut into thin strips. Reduce oven temperature to 400°F.

Remove the dough from the refrigerator, roll it out and transfer it into a 9-inch buttered tart pan. Pre-bake in the oven for 15 minutes and then remove.

Crumble the chèvre and combine it in a bowl with the egg, crème fraîche and honey. Pour into the crust and smooth out the surface. Return tart to the oven and bake for another 15–20 minutes until golden-brown.

While the tart cooks, toast pine nuts in an ungreased pan while stirring constantly until golden. Remove tart from the oven. Sprinkle with pine nuts and arrange pepper strips on top in a starburst pattern.

Hot or cold, this tart is always delicious.

This tart is excellent served with a typical Alsace Pinot Gris or an old, semi-dry Rheingau Riesling. The tannins in red wines tend to be incompatible with this dish.

Swiss Fondue

1 clove garlic,
2$^1/_2$ pounds Swiss fondue cheese,
1$^1/_2$ cups dry white wine,
1$^1/_2$ tablespoons cherry brandy,
1 teaspoon cornstarch,
Freshly ground white pepper,
Freshly grated nutmeg,
1–2 sweet or sour baguettes

Peel garlic, cut in half and rub vigorously around the inside of the fondue pot. Cut cheese into small cubes and place in the pot with the wine. Bring to a boil while stirring until the cheese is completely melted. Stir brandy and cornstarch together, then add to the cheese. Briefly return to a boil, then season with white pepper and nutmeg.

Cut the baguettes into bite-sized cubes and serve with the fondue.

Throughout the meal, simmer fondue on a warmer with adjustable heat. Always stir the speared bread cubes down around the bottom of the pot so the cheese stays creamy and doesn't burn.

In Switzerland, cheese fondue is made in a shallow saucepan with a handle made of glazed ceramic or thick glazed cast iron, called a "caquelon."

Almost every region in Switzerland prepares this convivial national dish using a unique cheese mixture. In Neuchâtel, they mix equal parts Gruyère and Emmenthaler; in Vaud, they use 1 pound Gruyère and ½ pound raclette; in Jura, they combine Gruyère and Tête de Moine; and in the Fribourg area, they like to eat fondue moitié-moitié (half and half) with equal parts Gruyère and Vacherin Fribourgeois. Try different combinations and discover your own favorite!

The quintessential fondue wine is a Swiss Fendant or Chasselas. A mature red Burgundy makes a divine match as well.

Fonduta

10 ounces fontina, 1½ cups milk,
3 egg yolks, 3 tablespoons melted butter,
Freshly ground white pepper,
4–8 slices Italian bread

Finely dice fontina. Transfer to a bowl and cover with
½ cup milk. Soak for several hours or overnight.

Using a double boiler, melt the cheese-milk mixture
over low heat. Whisk together egg yolks and remaining
milk and slowly stir into the cheese. Continue stirring
until the mixture thickens slightly, then stir in melted
butter and season with pepper.

To serve, ladle into warm soup bowls. Toast bread and
serve on the side.

If budget isn't an issue....In Piedmont, this simple
treat is topped with white Alba truffles shaved over
the top.

Aromatic Moscato wines are a perfect match
for fonduta. As a red wine, try a fruity, smooth
Dolcetto from the Piedmont region or a delicate
and aromatic Pinot Noir.

Chicory with Gruyère

4 heads chicory,
1⅓ cups heavy cream,
Freshly grated nutmeg,
5 ounces freshly grated Gruyère,
Kosher salt, Freshly ground white pepper

Preheat oven to 425°F.

Clean chicory, remove roots and cut out the bitter core
in a wedge shape. Cut heads in half lengthwise and
place in a cast iron or heavy pan. Add just enough
cream to cover chicory and season with a little nutmeg,
salt and pepper. Cover the pan and cook over low heat
for about 20 minutes.

Sprinkle the chicory with the Gruyère and bake in the
oven uncovered for about 10 minutes until golden-brown.

Served with crusty white bread, baked chicory is a
wonderful vegetarian entrée. In smaller portions,
it's a tasty side dish for hearty winter meals.

A mild Riesling goes well with this side dish. If served
with beef, pour a Merlot or Cabernet Sauvignon.

Cheese Spätzle

1 cup flour, 1½ tablespoons semolina, 2 eggs,
1 small onion, ½ cup butter, 2 bunches chives,
8 ounces freshly grated Emmenthaler,
Kosher salt, Freshly ground white pepper

In a bowl, mix flour, semolina, a pinch of salt and eggs
to form a runny batter (add a little water if necessary).
Beat vigorously with a wooden spoon until bubbles
form. In a large, wide pot, bring a large amount of
salted water to a boil.

Peel onions and cut into fine rings. In a large pan, heat
butter and sauté onions until tender but not brown.
Rinse chives and chop finely.

As soon as the water boils, let spätzle drop directly
from a spätzle grater into the water and stir—making
sure the water boils the whole time! When the spätzle

floats to the surface, it is done. Remove with a slotted spoon and drain on paper towels.

In a bowl, alternate layers of spätzle and cheese, seasoning each layer with pepper. Continue until all the spätzle has been used. Finally, pour sautéed onions over the spätzle and sprinkle generously with chives. Serve hot.

Cheese Spätzle is delicious with a crisp mâche salad.

Spätzle is best when made with spätzle flour. If spätzle flour is used, leave out the semolina.

A spätzle grater is an economical appliance that allows you to produce mountains of the most delicious "button" spätzle with a mere flick of the wrist.

A Blauer Zweigelt from Austria is by far the best wine match! Or for a domestic wine, sip an Old Vine Zinfandel with your spätzle.

Pasta Pockets with Herbs and Cheese

For the filling: $1/3$ pound russet potatoes,
2 ounces Parmigiano-Reggiano,
1 bunch chives, $2/3$ cup ricotta cheese,
2–3 tablespoons grappa
For the pasta dough: $2/3$ cup white flour,
$2/3$ cup rye flour
Plus: 1 onion, $1/2$ cup butter,
2 tablespoons chopped walnuts,
$1/2$ cup grated Emmenthaler,
2 tablespoons chopped Italian parsley,
Kosher salt, Freshly ground pepper

For the filling: Boil potatoes in salted water for 15–20 minutes. Finely grate Parmigiano-Reggiano. Rinse chives, pat dry and chop. Drain potatoes, peel, put through a ricer while hot and place in a bowl. Mix the potatoes with Parmigiano-Reggiano, chives, ricotta and grappa, and season with salt and pepper.

For the pasta dough: Heap flour on a work surface and form a well in the center. Pour in $3/4$ cup water and a pinch of salt and knead together to form a smooth dough. The dough should be more elastic than pasta dough but not sticking to your hands. Add a little more water if necessary. Shape the dough into a ball, brush with oil and let stand in a bowl for 30 minutes.

With a rolling pin, roll the dough out on a floured work surface, or roll out a thin sheet using a pasta maker and cut out 3 inch circles. Place 1 teaspoon of filling in the center of each circle, fold over the dough and press edges together to form crescent-shaped pockets. Crimp the round edge with a fork. Let dry on a floured work surface for 1 hour.

Peel the onion, dice finely and sauté in butter until light-brown. Add walnuts and heat until foamy.

Transfer pasta to a large pot of simmering, salted water and cook gently over low heat until they rise to the surface (about 3–5 minutes). Remove with a slotted spoon, drain and layer in a warm bowl. Top each layer with a little walnut butter and cheese. Sprinkle parsley over the top. Serve hot.

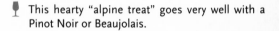 This hearty "alpine treat" goes very well with a Pinot Noir or Beaujolais.

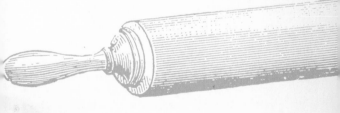

Meat and Seafood Entrées

In addition to the vegetarian entrées that were introduced in the previous chapter, the combination of cheese and meat or cheese and seafood has also inspired the world's chefs. This chapter includes a small sample from this broad category, which ranges from Veal Cordon Bleu to a tastefully seasoned Chicken Parmesan to Grilled Swordfish with Salsa.

If a meat or seafood dish with cheese is part of your menu, take subsequent courses into account when choosing the wine. If the entrée is to be followed by another dish with strong flavors, increase the intensity of the wine. Wine served with the cheese course must be at least as powerful as the wine served with the previous course.

Veal Cordon Bleu

4 veal cutlets (have the butcher cut a pocket in each),
Pinch of paprika, 4 slices cooked ham,
4 slices Swiss Emmenthaler, 1 egg, $1/2$ cup flour,
$1/2$ cup breadcrumbs, Olive oil for frying,
Kosher salt, Freshly ground black pepper

Rinse the veal, pat dry and season with salt, pepper and paprika. Fill each cutlet with 1 slice of ham and 1 slice of cheese and press closed.

In a shallow bowl, whisk the egg. Place flour and breadcrumbs in 2 more shallow bowls. Dredge the cutlets in flour, then in egg and finally in breadcrumbs. Press breading firmly onto the veal.

In a large pan, heat the olive oil and fry the veal on both sides for 3–4 minutes until crispy and brown. Remove and drain on paper towels.

Serve veal cutlets with a crisp green salad and peas.

Instead of veal cutlets, substitute chicken or turkey breast.

Either a Chianti or Sangiovese will do a good job to balance the oil in this dish while not overpowering the veal.

Baked Veal Cutlets

5 ounces freshly grated Comté (may substitute
Gruyère), 1 egg, 2 tablespoons crème fraîche,
Freshly grated nutmeg, 2 tablespoons butter,
4 veal cutlets, Kosher salt,
Freshly ground black pepper

Preheat oven to 450°F.

In a bowl, combine cheese, egg and crème fraîche and
season with salt, pepper and nutmeg.

In a large pan, heat the butter and fry veal on each side
for 3 minutes until halfway done. Place in a baking dish,
sprinkle cheese on top and drizzle with pan drippings.
Bake in the oven for 15 minutes until golden-brown.

Serve veal cutlets with a warm, crispy baguette or
noodles with browned butter.

A young Beaujolais or dry, cold, white wine are
highly compatible with the tender veal and mildly
aromatic Comté.

Involtini

8 thin veal cutlets (about 3 ounces each),
1 tablespoon extra virgin olive oil,
2 garlic cloves, 8 thin slices bacon,
2 tablespoons freshly grated Parmigiano-Reggiano,
1 ball mozzarella (4–5 ounces),
10–12 fresh sage leaves, Flour for dusting,
$\frac{1}{4}$ cup butter, $\frac{1}{2}$ cup white wine,
$\frac{1}{2}$ cup veal or beef stock,
1 tablespoon lemon juice, Kosher salt,
Freshly ground black pepper, Toothpicks

Pound the veal until very thin and brush one side with olive oil. Peel garlic, squeeze through a press and spread onto the veal. Top each with a slice of bacon and sprinkle with Parmigiano-Reggiano. Cut mozzarella into 8 strips and place on top. Grind a little pepper over the top and roll up the veal. Place a sage leaf on each roll, secure with a toothpick and dust the rolls with a thin layer of flour.

In a large pan, heat butter and brown veal rolls over moderate heat while turning until golden-brown. Season with salt and add the wine. Reduce by half and then add the stock. Cut remaining sage leaves into strips and add to the pan. Place the lid on the pan and braise for 12–15 minutes. Remove veal from the pan and keep warm.

Briefly bring sauce to a boil in the pan, season to taste with salt, pepper and lemon juice, and drizzle over the top of the veal.

Gnocchi and carrots make a great side dish with Involtini.

Chianti is a sound choice to drink with this meal. Or be a little daring and pour a fuller bodied Brunello or Sangiovese.

Beef Tenderloin Rossini

$^1/_2$ cup butter,
2 tablespoons extra virgin olive oil,
4 beef tenderloin fillets (5–6 ounces each),
$^1/_2$ tablespoon flour, $^1/_2$ cup semi-dry Madeira,
4 slices Gruyère, 4 slices air-dried ham,
$^1/_2$ cup béchamel sauce, $^1/_2$ cup veal or beef stock,
Kosher salt, Freshly ground black pepper

Preheat oven to 400°F.

In a pan, heat 2 tablespoons of butter and olive oil and brown beef fillets on both sides for 1 minute. Dust beef with a little flour and drizzle with a few drops of Madeira. Season on both sides with salt and pepper and continue braising for 2–3 minutes. Place the fillets in a baking dish and top each with 1 slice of cheese and 1 slice of ham. Spoon 1 tablespoon of béchamel sauce on top and bake in the oven for about 5 minutes.

Pour stock and remaining Madeira into the pan. Stir with a wooden spoon, scraping the residue off the bottom of the pan. Reduce to about $^1/_2$ cup and season with salt and pepper.

Remove beef from the oven and drizzle the sauce over the top before serving.

 Beef tenderloin is the perfect dish to serve with a mature Bordeaux or Burgundy with warm, velvety tannins and a harmonious balance of aromas.

Fillet of Beef with Gorgonzola Sauce

3 ounces Gorgonzola,
2 tablespoons extra virgin olive oil,
4 beef tenderloin fillets (5 ounces each),
1/2 cup dry white wine, 1/2 cup crème fraîche,
1 tablespoon lemon juice, Pinch of sugar,
Kosher salt, Freshly ground black pepper

Cut Gorgonzola into small pieces. In a heavy pan, heat the oil over very high heat. Sear the tenderloins on each side for 1 minute, reduce heat and fry for another 1–3 minutes on each side (rare, medium or well-done). Remove from the pan and keep warm.

Pour wine into pan residues. Add crème fraîche and Gorgonzola, stir with a wire whisk and reduce slightly. Season with lemon juice, sugar, salt and pepper. Return beef briefly to the pan and serve with the sauce on warm plates.

Beef tenderloin is delicious with fried chicory (see page 43) and a crispy baguette.

Serve a rich and tannic Cabernet Sauvignon or a complex, full-bodied Barolo with this meal for a truly satisfying experience.

Lamb and Feta Patties

1 large onion, 2 garlic cloves,
2 slices sandwich bread, 1 bunch Italian parsley,
1⅓ pounds ground lamb, 1 egg,
1½ teaspoons dried oregano,
½ teaspoon cumin, 7 ounces mild feta,
⅓ cup extra virgin olive oil,
Kosher salt, Freshly ground black pepper

Peel the onion and garlic and dice finely. Toast the bread, soak in a bowl of water and squeeze out the liquid. Finely chop parsley. In a bowl, combine onion, garlic, bread, parsley, lamb, egg and oregano. Season with salt, pepper and cumin. Knead thoroughly, divide into 8 equal portions and shape into patties ½ inch thick. Dice the feta and evenly place the pieces on top of four patties, cover with the other four patties and press together firmly around the edges.

In a large pan, heat the oil and fry patties on each side for 2–3 minutes.

Lamb patties go well with pita bread and a Greek salad.

Pair lamb patties with a Greek wine, such as a cold, slightly resinous Retsina or serve a crisp and earthy Sauvignon Blanc or, a rich, spicy Gewürztraminer.

Turkey Piccata with Mozzarella

1 pound turkey breast, 1 lemon,
$^1/_3$ cup extra virgin olive oil,
$^1/_2$ pound broccoli,
1–2 beefsteak tomatoes,
1 ball mozzarella (4 ounces),
1 tablespoon small capers, Kosher salt,
Freshly ground white pepper

Cut turkey breast on an angle into thin slices. Rub with pepper. Rinse the lemon under hot water and dry. Finely grate half the lemon peel and stir into 3 tablespoons of olive oil. Remove zest from remaining lemon half and set aside for garnish. Squeeze juice out of both lemon halves and set aside. Brush turkey with the lemon-oil mixture, cover and refrigerate for 1–2 hours.

Preheat oven to 325°F.

Clean broccoli and separate into florets. In a saucepan, bring 4 cups salted water to a boil and blanch broccoli at a rolling boil for 3 minutes. Rinse under cold water and drain well.

Remove cores from tomatoes and cut into thick slices. Cut mozzarella into thin slices. Top each slice of turkey with 1 slice of tomato and 1 slice of mozzarella and season with a little salt and pepper.

Transfer the turkey to a baking sheet, leaving adequate space between each slice and drizzle with remaining lemon marinade. Arrange broccoli in between the turkey and bake in the oven for 5 minutes.

Whisk together remaining olive oil and 2 tablespoons of lemon juice to make a foamy dressing. Stir in capers and season with salt and pepper.

Remove baking sheet from the oven. Drizzle the turkey and broccoli with lemon dressing and bake in the oven for another 5–10 minutes. Just before serving, sprinkle with a little lemon zest.

For something unique, pour a smooth French rosé, such as a Côtes de Provence. For a white, serve a strong bodied, fruity Chardonnay. And for a red, pour a Sangiovese—its acidity will unzip the flavor of the lemon and capers, but not overpower the turkey.

Chicken Parmesan

1 cup crème fraîche, 2 tablespoons butter,
12 ounces sliced mushrooms, 4 chicken breast fillets,
3¹/₂ ounces freshly grated Parmigiano-Reggiano,
Kosher salt, Freshly ground black pepper

Preheat oven to 400°F.

In a saucepan, reduce the crème fraîche over medium heat until smooth. Set aside. In a pan, melt the butter, brown the mushrooms and season with salt and pepper.

Rinse the chicken and pat dry. Season with salt and pepper and place in a greased baking dish. Spread the mushrooms on top of the chicken. Stir two-thirds of the Parmigiano-Reggiano into the crème fraîche and pour over the chicken. Sprinkle with the remaining Parmigiano-Reggiano and bake in the oven for 15–20 minutes until golden-brown.

Enjoy Chicken Parmesan with a crispy baguette and a green salad with creamy dressing.

For a red, pour a Pinot Noir or a Sangiovese. Sangiovese and mushrooms are a match made in heaven. If you're in the mood for white wine, drink a dry Chardonnay.

Baked Sole

4 cleaned, skinned sole fillets,
1/2 cup finely chopped Italian parsley,
1/2 cup breadcrumbs, 1 clove minced garlic,
1/3 cup extra virgin olive oil,
1/3 cup freshly grated young pecorino,
Kosher salt, Freshly ground black pepper

Preheat oven to 425°F.

Season the sole with salt and pepper and transfer to an oiled baking dish. Rinse parsley, dry and chop finely. Combine parsley, breadcrumbs, garlic and a little olive oil to form a paste and spread onto both sides of the fish. Sprinkle pecorino over the top. Drizzle the remaining olive oil over the sole and bake in the oven for 15 minutes.

Serve with warm ciabatta and lemon wedges.

A Pinot Grigio with its refreshing citrus undertones goes nicely with this dish as does a full-bodied Puilly Fuissé or Sauvignon Blanc.

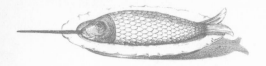

Grilled Swordfish with Salsa

For the swordfish:, 1 pound swordfish,
8 black olives, ½ cup grated provolone,
¼ cup breadcrumbs, 1–2 onions, 6–8 bay leaves

For the salsa: ½ cup boiling water, ½ cup olive oil,
1 tablespoon finely chopped Italian parsley,
1–2 teaspoons finely chopped capers,
½ teaspoon dried oregano,
Kosher salt, Freshly ground black pepper,
Wooden skewers

For the rolls: Rinse the swordfish, pat dry and season
with salt and pepper. Cut into thin rectangles of about
2 x 4 inches. Chop the olives finely and combine with
cheese and breadcrumbs. Spread in the middle of the
swordfish and roll up into rolls. Peel onions and slice.
Thread swordfish, onions and bay leaves onto wooden
skewers.

For the salsa: Combine water, olive oil, parsley and capers and season with oregano, salt and pepper.

Brush swordfish with salsa and cook on a charcoal grill, turning occasionally and brushing with salsa.

In southern Italy, grilled swordfish is very popular—which is why southern Italian wines go especially well with this summertime treat. Try a white Nuragus from Sicily, a white Apulian Locorotondo or a Calabrian Falanghina. A crisp Sauvignon Blanc will tame the salty and pungent nature of the capers and olives in the stuffing and sauce. If you're in the mood to go red, try a light Sangiovese or Chianti. Their fine fruit and acidity will hold its own with the flavors of the dish.

Cheese at the End of a Meal

For many gourmands, a small assortment of the finest cheeses is the preferred way to end a meal. An abundant cheese platter can actually replace a meal. Manchego with quince jelly or pecorino with pears and aged balsamic vinegar are best enjoyed alone. Such delicacies do not need to be preceded by an entire meal. Enjoy them as an afternoon snack or at a summer picnic. The next time you're tempted to grab a bag of chips, slice up a little Emmenthaler and a few walnuts for a change.

There are some wine and cheese combinations that are divinely inspired, chief among them being Stilton with port and Roquefort with Sauterne. Such perfect combinations in the case of a cheese platter, where the wine choice should always be based on the strongest cheese are hard to achieve. Be sure to adapt the cheese and wine combination at the end of your meal to be complementary with the preceding courses.

Cheese Paired with Wine

Following are several classic pairings. After sampling these suggestions, experiment with your own favorite cheese and wine varieties. Remember to take cheese out of the refrigerator about 1 hour before serving to allow its full aroma and flavors to unfold.

Pecorino with Pears and Aged Balsamic Vinegar

10 ounces fresh Pecorino Toscano,
1 large, firm pear (e.g., Bartlett),
1 small bunch arugula,
$1/2$–$1/3$ cup aged balsamic vinegar or balsamic vinegar reduction (see tip on page 23)

Cut the pecorino into coarse matchsticks. Peel the pear, remove its core and cut into similar size matchsticks. Rinse the arugula and dry.

Arrange the arugula onto 4 plates. Top with pecorino and pears and drizzle with balsamic vinegar.

🍷 Slowly sip a Vin Santo, the "holy wine" of Tuscany.

Swiss Emmenthaler with Walnuts

10 ounces Swiss Emmenthaler (cave-aged),
Several walnuts, Sourdough bread

Serve Emmenthaler on a board with walnuts and sliced bread.

Genuine cave-aged Emmenthaler is a masterpiece. Chew it slowly. Enjoy the mild and spicy aroma in exudes as it melts on your tongue and its long, nutty finish. The freshest walnuts intensify the flavor experience. Toasting walnuts also enhances their flavor.

A versatile Pinot Noir or Cabernet Sauvignon are both good matches for this cheese as a conclusion to a meal.

Parmigiano-Reggiano with Dark Bread

8 ounces Parmigiano-Reggiano,
Mildly salted butter,
1 loaf dark artisan bread

Arrange Parmigiano-Reggiano on a board with butter and sliced bread.

Crumbled or shaved, Parmigiano-Reggiano is fantastic with airy, dark wheat bread with a crispy crust.

For a wonderful and rare combination, serve this hard cheese with a fruity Chardonnay sparkling wine (Blanc de Blanc). If this pair seems too intense, you can't go wrong with a spicy, aromatic Pinot Noir or a Merlot.

Stilton and Port

Serves 6–8:

16 ounces Stilton, ²/₃ cup port wine

The day before serving, press Stilton into a suitable ceramic or clay container with a lid. Using a skewer or other pointed object, pierce a series of vertical holes all the way to the bottom of the container and fill with port. Cover and refrigerate overnight. When the wine has been completely absorbed, add more.

Stilton prepared this way has an incomparable flavor!

Port wine is the natural accompaniment to be served with Stilton. A very old, expertly aged port will provide a tremendously satisfying flavor experience.

Manchego and Quince Jelly

1 fresh red chile pepper,
10 ounces manchego,
$^1/_2$ cup quince jelly

Rinse chile pepper, cut in half lengthwise, remove stem, seeds and interior, and dice finely. Thinly slice manchego and arrange on 4 plates. Spoon 2 teaspoons of quince jelly onto each plate and sprinkle with a little chile pepper.

The savory spiciness of this cheese and the extreme sharpness of the chile pepper unite with the tart sweetness of the quince jelly to form a unique whole. The Spanish like to serve this combination with a semi-dry sherry or a rosado.

Munster and Caraway Seeds

10 ounces ripe Munster,
2 teaspoons caraway seeds,
Fresh, crusty, sour baguette

Arrange cheese on 4 plates and sprinkle each portion with $^1/_2$ teaspoon caraway seeds. Serve baguette sliced on the side.

The beloved Alsace Munster smells unbelievably strong but tastes incomparably mild and spicy; especially (and as is recommended) without the rind and not overly aged. In Alsace, there is also a young version that is like feta and is great crumbled over salad. The fine, slightly sweet spiciness of the caraway seeds complements Munster's flavor perfectly.

Alsace winegrowers produce the ideal match for this specialty. A Riesling or Gewürztraminer provides perfect enjoyment. A very young Munster is also compatible with the flowery fruit of a Muscat d'Alsace.

Tête de Moine and Figs

4 ripe figs, Freshly ground pepper,
2–3 tablespoons port wine,
8 ounces Tête de Moine (as rosettes),
Several walnuts

Carefully rinse figs and pat dry. Slice and season with a little pepper. Pour port on top and let stand for about 10 minutes. Drain figs on paper towels and arrange onto 4 plates. Arrange Tête de Moine rosettes alongside the figs and sprinkle with walnuts.

Tête de Moine is pared into beautiful rosettes with the aid of a "Girolle," a special device on which the cheese is skewered and pared off in lovely "blossoms." Whether the shape of this cheese actually resembles a monk's head as the name implies is a matter of opinion.

Tête de Moine tastes best when fresh; then it's wonderful with a sumptuous Chasselas. For a special combination, pair this mild and spicy cheese with a fragrant Blanc de Noir from the Lake of Neuchâtel.

Baked Vacherin Mont d'Or

1 whole Vacherin Mont d'Or cheese in a wooden box,
½ cup Pinot Gris or Gewürztraminer,
Fresh baguette cut into cubes

Preheat oven to 400°F.

Remove the lid from the box, leaving the cheese inside. Using a skewer, make about 20 deep holes in the cheese. Carefully pour in the wine and bake the cheese in the oven. After 10–12 minutes, the cheese should be soft and the wine absorbed. Just before serving, fold back the top rind.

Dip bread cubes into the soft and aromatic cheese pâté for a heavenly experience!

This cheese was made to be served with a Pinot Gris or a delicately sweet Gewürztraminer.

Cheese Platter Basics

Whether for a holiday feast or a casual meal with friends, a respectable selection of cheeses provides a satisfactory ending to any meal. Follow a few rules and your cheese platter is guaranteed to be a success. Be sure that the individual cheeses are optimally aged and served at room temperature and you won't have to be overly concerned about the particular varieties. Let your motto be "Less is More." Although there are an estimated 3000 varieties of cheese in the world, the successful cheese platter is more a matter of quality than quantity. On a buffet serving a crowd, you're covered with 8–10 varieties of cheese. After a nice meal, offer up to 3–5 cheese types and count on 2–3 ounces per person.

Choosing Made Easy

Because most cheese can be placed in one of five categories (hard, semi-hard, semi-soft, fresh and blue), making choices for your cheese platter is easy: Try to pick a representative from each group. Depending on your preferences, you can compose a rich, mild or spicy cheese platter. Generally, mild varieties are more suitable for a brunch or afternoon, whereas their hard companions tend to emerge after dark.

Mild Cheese Platter

A mild cheese platter may include Montagnolo, Assagio Pressato, Formai de Mut, Bel Paese, Gèramont, young Gouda, Illertaler, Majorero and Chavroux. Most of these cheeses are compatible with white or red wines, such as a Chardonnay or Chianti.

Classic Cheese Assortment

A classic cheese assortment like the one rolled out on a cheese cart in restaurants, combines a variety of cheeses ranging from mild to rich and should be eaten in this order. For example, serve the following combination as a small but delicious cheese platter at the end of a meal: Chèvre frais, Camembert de Normandie, Saint Nectaire, Tomme de Savoie and Bleu d'Auvergne. These cheeses are ideal with a rich, ripe Pommerol or a sweet white wine such as a Jurançon or Muscato.

The first step to making cheese selections is to choose a specific theme. For instance, compose a platter on the basis of country. Besides France, very good cheese is also made in Italy, Switzerland, Austria, Spain and the United States. Or choose your cheese by region, such as Alpine cheeses, cheese from Burgundy or Normandy or even from California. A cheese platter can also be composed on the basis of different degrees of ripeness. For example, a series of Goudas ranging from very young to very old can be exciting. You could even try this combination with a Dutch Riesling for a truly regional tasting.

Be sure to make your platter a feast for the eyes as well. Cheese comes in a wide variety of shapes and colors. Compose your cheese platter based on sight. Pyramids, cylinders, rounds and squares in red, yellow, white and black are much more appealing than five pale yellow, uniform round cheeses, no matter how good they taste!

Nothing But Cheese?

Bread, too, of course! Fresh bread is part of every cheese assortment. Generally speaking, the bread should be neutral, such as a crusty baguette or ciabatta. Sometimes, a walnut bread is appropriate (for example, with a nutty Emmenthaler) or even raisin or fruit bread (with a sweet, fresh Gouda) and regular or dark pumpernickel (with hearty semi-hard, semi-soft and blue cheeses).

The small selection of cheeses that closes a meal can be garnished with grapes, apples or pear wedges. A large cheese platter can include dried fruit, such as figs, dates, apricots and raisins. Depending on your choice of cheese, consider serving green onions, radishes or olives.

Wine Selection

Since a cheese platter is a combination of different cheeses with different flavors, wine selection is actually quite simple. Base the selection on the strongest cheese. There are no hard and fast recommendations to be followed because, again, personal preference will be your guide. Consider the context in which the cheese will be consumed. With brunch, serve a light champagne. For a midday snack, serve a rosé, fruity white or lighter red. In the evening, something heavier like a Burgundy would be appropriate.

If you keep in mind some of these basic guidelines when planning your get together or event and add a healthy dose of your own taste, your experience is sure to be enjoyable.

In the spirit of entertaining, Cheers!

Little Cheese and Wine Glossary

The following is a list of some of the terms used in connection with wine and cheese. The list makes no claim to completeness, but it is a healthy start.

Cheese

Affinage	The process of aging cheese to the optimal degree of ripeness.
Casein	The principle protein in cow's milk that is produced for cheese making.
Cheese cultures	Totality of microorganisms present on the rind or in the pâté during the cheese's ripening phase.
Clots	Coagulated, curdled milk.
Coagulation	Rennet or lactic acid cultures are added to the milk to cause it to curdle.
Curd	Curdled milk that has separated into solid and liquid components.
Dry matter	All of the components of cheese minus the moisture.
Enzymes	Special proteins that play an important role in cheese production (for example, in conjunction with the fermentation that turns lactose into lactic acid). They make significant contributions to the formation of aroma and flavor.
FDM	Acronym for fat in the dry matter.
Lactic acid bacteria	Microorganisms that ferment the lactose to produce flavoring substances.

Pasteurization	Process of briefly heating to 70–72°C (e.g., raw milk for cheese production).
Pâté	The interior of the cheese.
Piercing	Puncturing the cheese with needles when producing green- and blue-veined cheese to introduce the air necessary for mold formation.
Raw-milk cheese	Cheese made from unpasteurized milk.
Rennet	An enzyme obtained from a calf's stomach and used to coagulate the milk.
Rind	Protective surface on cheese.
Whey	The nonfat liquid that separates from the curds during cheese production.

Wine

AOC	Appellation d'origine contrôlée— "appellation of controlled origin," applied to quality French wines.
Balanced	A wine that demonstrates a harmonious relationship among all its elements.
Barrique	225-liter oak cask that gives wine very pronounced woody tones.
Character	Distinctive personality of a wine based on the variety, soil, climate and fermentation.
Cloying	A wine with too much sugar in relation to its acidity.
Developed	A wine that has reached the peak of its maturity.

DOC/DOCG | Denominazione di origine controllata (e garantita)—"controlled denomination of origin," applied to quality Italian wines. DOC (Denominación de Origen) also designates quality Spanish wines.

Dry | A wine without residual sugar.

Extract | Contents of the grape juice minus the liquid component.

Fermentation | The methods used to age wine (e.g., in steel tanks or barrels).

Finish | The flavors that remain on the palate after a wine is swallowed.

Mellow | Subtle aromas, soft and elegant.

Must weight | The amount of sugar in unfermented grape juice.

Noble rot | Late-harvested (= sweet) grapes develop the beneficial mold (*Botrytis cinerea*) to produce a powerfully concentrated wine with an unmistakable flavor and aroma.

Oechsle scale | Device for measuring the specific gravity of grape must (oechsle level) to derive its sugar content. Used in Germany, Switzerland and Luxembourg.

QbA | Quality wine from a specific German region. Other quality levels stipulated in the German Wine Law are Kabinett, Spätlese, Auslese, Beerenauslese, Trockenbeeren- nauslese and Eiswein. The wines of each region and each grape variety are classified according to the precisely defined minimum

	specific gravities (unit of measurement is the "oechsle level") of the must.
Residual sugar	Unfermented sugar contained in a wine already bottled.
Rich	A hearty, full-bodied wine that stimulates all the taste buds.
Round	A full-bodied wine with a high-alcohol level.
Smooth & Soft	Designates wine that is low in acidity.
Spicy	Intensely aromatic and flavorful wine with fruity nuances resembling spices.
Supple	A lighter-bodied wine that is extremely pleasing to drink.
Tannins	General term for tannic acids. In wine it comes from the grape skins and contributes significantly to flavor formation and aging. Good, storable red wines must start off containing a lot of tannins, which break down over time or react with other flavoring ingredients, resulting in the wine's maturation.
Tart	Very high in acid, generally refers to the flavor that creates a pucker sensation in the mouth.
Thin	A wine lacking body that seems watered down.
Toasted	Barrel interiors are toasted to a greater or lesser degree, for a subsequent effect on the flavor of the wine.

List of Recipes

Appetizers

Vegetarian Entrées

Meat and Seafood Entrées

Cheese at the End of a Meal